Originally,

THE
EVOLUTIONARY GUIDEBOOK

FOLLOW YOUR HEART
BE YOUR POWER

Copyright © 2016 by Mr. E. Dan Smith III

All rights reserved. This book may not be reproduced in whole or in part without written permission from the publisher, except by a reviewer who may quote brief passages in a review; nor may any part of this book be reproduced, stored in a retrieval system, or transmitted in any form or by any means, electronic, mechanical, photocopying, recording, or other, without written permission from the publisher.

Library of Congress
Cataloging-in-Publication Data Available
The Evolutionary Guidebook
MysterE

ISBN 978-0-9719761-4-6

Published by EaseUp Life is Heart
Boulder, CO 80305

Editorial:
Cover: Dustin Brunson
Proofreader: Miranda Dow Miller
Labyrinth Illustrations: MysterE
Special Appreciation: B Gotwald
Printed in the United States of America

Contents

Seven Labyrinths for One	i
The 8 Evolutionary Guidelines	ii
Evolutionary Guideline Essences	iii
Introduction	1
Guideline One	8
Guideline Two	20
Guideline Three	32
Guideline Four	46
Guideline Five	60
Guideline Six	74
Guideline Seven	90
Guideline Eight	104

Seven Labyrinths for One…

Portal of Awakening

©2014 MysterE Designs

The 8 Evolutionary Guidelines

Allow Life to Come to You, *And Act from Intuitive Feeling.*	One
What You Require to Evolve Shows Up Perfectly, *As You Are in Step with Evolution.*	Two
Be Light. Light Is Light. *Lightness Spreads Light.*	Three
Be in the Silence. Silence is the Doorway. *Become a Noise Reducer.*	Four
Simplicity Frees Energy. Simplify Everything *So Purity Can Work with Purity.*	Five
Rapid Acceleration Occurs When People *Get into Evolutionary Flow Together.*	Six
Dive into the Mystery—Into Not Knowing *And Become What Wants To Happen.*	Seven
See Perfection Now – For Only Perfection Exists. *What is Happening Now is Divine Orchestration.*	Eight

Evolutionary Guideline Essences

One   *Willingness*

Two   *Appreciation*

Three   *Allowance*

Four   *Neutrality*

Five   *Initiation*

Six   *Efficiency*

Seven   *Nothingness*

Eight   *Alchemy*

Beyond Any Emotion is the Vibration of Pure Love.

Pure Love is the Foundation of the Universe.

Coming into Relationship with this Vibration is the Key to Becoming Your Evolutionary Potential.

Guideline Introduction:

Within everyone is the capacity to be a powerful center for change—vast sweeping change. Not by changing oneself, but by stepping into one's evolutionary potential to *become* change.

We are <u>not</u> separate from our environment. Everything, including us, in spiritual and physical form, is simply a part of the universal evolving ecology.

All we require to be in our potential is simply to *come into step with evolution—to simply become what is already happening and changing.* By doing so we are able to flow peacefully within the river of the changing landscape and clearly see how to interact with life. This frees enormous energy to channel into life purpose and meaning.

We have lived in an age of evolutionary contradiction in which everything has continued to evolve—yet people have invested their happiness and security into institutions and relationships for stability and predictability as if they were insulated from change. As long as these institutions have held, people have felt powerful and in control of their circumstances.

But these institutions of finance, religion, education, government, and marriage - were built as permanent fixtures on the ever-shifting sands of evolution itself. Hence, they have become weathered and weakened like a crumbling sidewalk, causing people to feel unsettled and out of sync.

What is happening right now cannot be completely understood by the human mind, but one thing is clear: The rules we created to live our lives by are changing, even disintegrating. What used to work well no longer does and may become obsolete in the near future.

Evolution is about continual adaptation, and to thrive, we must come into harmony with change. We must come into alignment with what is already happening rather than with what we want to happen.

In a world that has more than enough resources for everyone, and within an environment whose fragility is becoming increasingly apparent, evolution's track is inevitable.

Evolution is quickening its pace and guiding us through a cultural transition to set aside our individual needs to hold a higher, more inclusive vision for ourselves and the planet.

We are each being tapped on the shoulder—to live with a new sense of awareness and interconnectedness and to start relying on intuition and feelings in ways we could not have done before. We are being asked to experience life through the heart and answer its call of self-reliance, universal compassion, and purposeful living.

The small reward is we can quickly come into harmony with what wants to happen for our lives. We can become authentically empowered and live our fullest potential.

The larger reward is we each become a powerful center for change that impacts the people around us as they tap into our evolutionary state and then their own potential. This adds velocity to the global transition of becoming a more heart-centered and therefore, sustainable planet.

The Evolutionary Guidelines facilitate the transition to becoming one's own evolutionary guide by offering a simple map to help each one of us drop into the heart as the focal point of awareness.

Why Guidelines—and not rules?

Rules demand compliance, whereas guidelines provide direction. The transition to becoming heart-centered is a process of leaving behind the ideals of right versus wrong and good versus bad to embrace a more centered and balanced approach to life.

It is about being in harmony with what is being presented to you at any given time rather than becoming polarized or motivated by moral code, social expectations, and personal security.

Life becomes much simpler. It becomes about being in step with your evolution, or not.

The 8 Evolutionary Guidelines offered in the following chapters are just that—*guidelines*.

They show us how to be "in-step" with evolution and therefore our potential.

They show us how to save valuable energy and vitality that can be utilized for creating what is really important to the well-being for all people, including us. They hold no power over anyone.

They are simply suggestions for where and how to interact with what is already happening in a much more efficient and self-reliant way. They teach us how to relate to everything in our lives differently. Simply put, they show us how to be in the flow our heart's desire and not get lost.

All of us are evolving—there is not anything we can do about that. However, when we come more "into step" with evolution, we enter a slipstream of energy that fundamentally changes how we interact with life, moment-to-moment and day-to-day.

The result of being in step is a heightened state of awareness and the ability to be more centered and joyful regardless of our life circumstances.

We gain the ability to easefully channel energy into life purpose and service. We are connected to magic, flow, serendipity and grace.

Being in step with evolution is like the difference between riding a steam locomotive and a bullet train. Both are heading in the same direction, but everyone who can, chooses to ride the speeding train.

Evolutionary Guideline One

*Allow Life to Come to You,
And Act from Intuitive Feeling.*

Guideline Essence: *Willingness*

Most of what has happened and what is taught today in human development is oriented in the expression of willpower and then gauged by some measure of achievement and success.

The corresponding directive usually has something to do with, "*What do I want and how can I best go about getting it?*"

Western culture is permeated with the concept of using the *law of attraction* as a means to getting what you want. This interpretation of the law of attraction is that "like attracts like" and it can be used to create almost anything a person desires—namely wealth, success, and relationships. The popular application of the law is for people to try to manage their thoughts, feelings, and actions to attract the life circumstances they desire.

This method has allowed people to achieve remarkable things. However, following that approach today is an ultimate hindrance to living your evolutionary potential because something else is happening for a greater collective benefit that requires our attention. We are living in a new age of human possibility—an age that demands an evolved compassionate approach to working with the law of attraction.

The law of attraction describes a very powerful force indeed. It is a force of consciousness that is continually in play without your active involvement.

It easefully connects you to experiences, people, ideas, and situations enabling you to evolve and grow into higher expressions of life based on the vibration of your attractor state.

Everyone has an attractor state; it's simply your life force – a summation of your vibration. It is an energetic mosaic of all your thoughts, feelings, and karma, interwoven with your soul's blueprint for the highest expression of life.

When you are *actively* attempting to influence your attractor state, you are expending vital energy that contradicts what is already *naturally* occurring for your highest good. On the contrary, when you are willing to be in harmony with the vibration of your attractor state, you free yourself to live in potential today.

Take a moment right now and imagine that indeed the law of attraction is naturally and perfectly bringing forth your highest expression of life.

In other words, you are being offered every-thing, every-one, every-situation, every-feeling, and every-thought you require to be perfectly in step with your evolutionary potential *and* no additional effort is required to change your attractor state.

Imagine right now, despite your contrary ideas, feelings, and resistance to what you are experiencing in life and reading here—***everything*** in your midst is exactly in alignment with who you have the potential to become. Life has, in fact, come to you perfectly.

Would this change the way you engage with life?

Feel into this possibility for a moment. You would never complain about anything. Likewise, you would not become angry, jealous, fearful, or self-righteous. You would not be in a hurry, stretch the truth, or punish a child.

You would not feel obligated to work harder than others or blame anyone for your shortcomings. You would not compare yourself to, or compete against anyone. You would never want or need to be anywhere other than where you are right now. You could begin to appreciate everything in your life without a reason to judge it as useful, good, or right.

How much energy would be left over after making such a wholesale change? How could that energy be used? What would be the impact?

The simple answer is it would free an unquantifiable amount of energy, which would be utilized in a multitude of ways to create self-reliance, facilitate personal healing, and formulate the expression of life purpose.

In short, it would bring about an accelerated life track by bringing your gift to light.

In this evolutionary age, the force the law of attraction attempts to describe is not best utilized as some outside force to be quarantined for your personal benefit. It is something inherently within your awareness to be appreciated as a perfect element of evolutionary design for emerging potential for a more compassionate existence for all human beings.

It is to be enjoyed as always working with your attractor state to bring to you exactly what you require, at exactly the perfect time and place, including what needs to be healed, transcended, acted upon, and explored.

It is to be seen as a vehicle guiding you toward your highest potential as long as you are willing to come into step with evolution, set intentions and take intuitive action.

So what is being "in step" or "out of step" with evolution?

When you are in resistance (emotional or otherwise) with what is showing up in your life, you are out of step with evolution because you are operating against natural law. Your attractor state continues to attract the experiences you avoid by reinforcing an existing mosaic.

For example, when you attract the same type of relationship (or situation) repeatedly and you respond with resistance or frustration because you really want something different, you are reinvesting this reaction back into your attractor state and inviting more of the same. This keeps you stuck in a pattern until you learn to engage differently with what life is bringing you.

Likewise, by spending valuable energy managing your thoughts, feelings and actions to create a new relationship (or situation) from a place of need, you are also out of step because you are working in contradiction to your soul's evolutionary design.

You are trying to go in one direction, but there are forces at work behind the veils of limited awareness.

It is literally like being tethered by an invisible rubber band that either snaps or pulls you back when misguided willpower has faded.

Therefore <u>being **out-of-step** with evolution is defined as</u>: to be in resistance in any form—in thought, feeling, word or action—to what you are being presented with at any moment.

Alternatively, when you are in a state of *willingness* to be with whatever comes into your life (neither accepting nor rejecting), you are more fully in step with your evolution because you are now in harmony with what life is bringing you. Willingness frees energy.

Within *willingness*, your attractor state is free of resistance and becomes centered in the heart. Your entire energetic body refines and expands into a higher frequency.

This allows you to experience higher states of awareness to better witness the evolutionary forces at play. You can actually experience a space between what you have been experiencing and what you are to evolve into, enabling you to listen and feel into your intuition in a new way. You gain access to your inner evolutionary guide.

From the position of evolutionary guide, you immediately empower your self to set powerful intentions to accelerate your life.

Therefore, <u>being **in-step** with evolution is defined as</u>: Saying yes. Saying yes to being in your heart with what is happening in life, causing an expanded state of awareness from which your intuitive voice clearly guides you in setting intentions and taking action to be in evolutionary harmony with the law of attraction.

So, how can I step into my evolution more fully now?

Simply begin gently incorporating the 8 Evolutionary Guidelines into your life—starting with Evolutionary Guideline One:

Allow Life to Come to You, and Act from Intuitive Feeling.

Give yourself permission to slow the pace of your life and pay more attention to the feelings inside you by dropping your awareness into the heart. Train yourself to pause before taking any new action and feel into your awareness before making decisions.

Most people are so busy they are missing beautiful opportunities every day to step into life in new and empowering ways. A very small shift in the way you live can pay enormous dividends.

As you gain the experience of slowing down and listening to your intuition, you begin to trust that it guides you efficiently and with care.

You learn to have faith that everything coming into your life is there to help you evolve. You are amazed how much energy is left over from this new way of creating your life and how it can be used in more empowering ways.

Guideline Action One: *Slow Down*

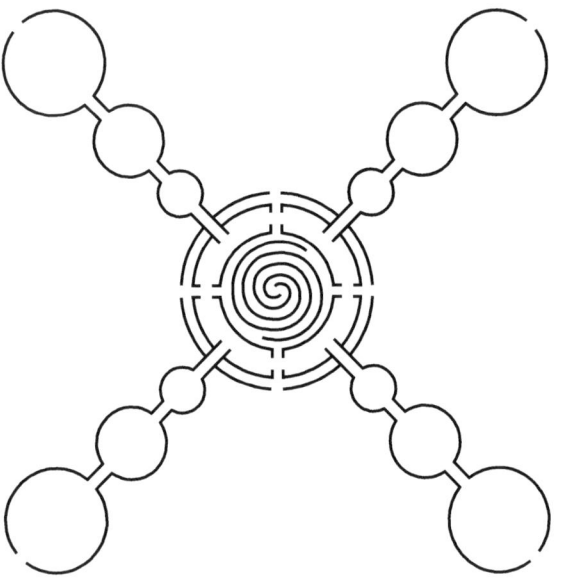

Evolutionary Guideline Two

*What You Require to Evolve
Shows Up Perfectly,
As You Are In-Step with Evolution.*

Guideline Essence: *Appreciation*

Tremendous amounts of energy and vitality are expended by people every day in attempts to manage perceptions. *What does she think of me? I hope no one will notice. Look at what I'm doing. I'm just going to go along with what they want so I don't rock the boat.*

This blanket of illusion in which we cloak ourselves is an attempt to insulate from discomfort. We hope that by holding up a façade of how we would like things to be, we can buffer ourselves from feeling anything that makes us uncomfortable. So we bend the truth, jump to conclusions, hold judgments, and create fantasies in hopes of keeping life predictable and safe, while we are, in effect, barricading ourselves behind a mirage.

Perceptions are born of self-judgment. To present something different than your authentic self takes vast amounts of energy. The illusion is unsustainable and keeps you from being in sync with what wants to happen in your life. To manage perception of your experience detracts from the vibrancy of your attractor state and scatters your vitality rather than concentrating it into the power of your authentic self.

Managing perceptions is in opposition to your evolution because your power gravitates away from reality toward something without foundational truth.

To be authentic is to interact more fully with the energy of change by being transparent and real. This is the path of the evolutionary—to free yourself from judgment and misrepresentation and enter a state of appreciation.

To be in appreciation is a great catalyst of evolutionary flow, because it is impossible to be in appreciation and to manage perceptions simultaneously. They are different energetic frequencies.

Holding perceptions is a contracted and heavier energy of fear and is held in the mind. Being in a state of appreciation is a lighter, more freeing energy found in the heart.

To be in appreciation is to become so filled with the wonder and awe of the majesty and mystery of impermanent life that you lose interest in managing perceptions.

Appreciation is to be beyond the emotional level of human love and to be immersed in the vibration of divine love. It is to move beyond what tethers you - into freedom.

When in genuine appreciation, you feel a deep knowing that even though you cannot see beyond the next bend in the river, everything required for the journey of life simply shows up. When you trust the evolutionary flow in this way, you are naturally inspired to speak your truth. When all your words and thoughts line up in the same direction of truth, they become as strong as ocean currents because there is no resistance from trying to manipulate perceptions. This free flow further accelerates your evolution. It is like removing trash and debris from a stream so the water can flow more directly and freely.

By conserving the energy you formerly placed on managing perceptions, you become a more conscious, creative participant in how your life evolves. This new level of personal empowerment helps you step more fully into an evolutionary flow.

So how does this help me evolve, exactly?

To be evolving is literally to be in harmony with the energy of evolution. It is a way of freely interacting with this energy to naturally increase the vibrancy of your attractor state. By appreciating everything in your experience and letting go of maintaining mental constructs, you transfer power to your heart.

Each moment is an evolutionary moment, bringing to you new opportunities to be in step or not. Your responsibility is merely to choose to flow freely with your experience.

When you are willing to live this way, you begin to experience synchronicity and flow. You notice everything is already working with more fluidity and far more ease and grace than you previously understood.

The appreciation of the moment itself, without the static energy of maintaining a veil of perception, brings color, beauty and vibrancy to your experience and opens a slower, more conscious pace of life.

When you are in alignment with the energy of evolution, what you require at any moment simply appears. Thoughts frequently manifest into form, people show up at exactly the right time, and genius ideas for the advancement of your heart's desires are birthed. You become aware that your intuition is much more than a fleeting knowingness and you recognize an ever-present open channel to higher states of consciousness – accessible through your open heart.

From here, it is easy to become expectant that this type of flow is the way of your evolutionary path. You begin to believe life should always be exciting and match your desires. Everything is working out just the way you wanted, and this is the way it should always be.

This is where it becomes easy to fall out of step, because you are asking to come into step with an evolving universe. This evolving universe is benevolently bringing you *everything* you require to evolve perfectly, especially what is difficult and needs to be healed and/or transcended to fully bring out your gift.

The law of attraction is not discriminating with what it brings to you, so to be in step with evolution you must not be discriminating with how you relate to what you receive.

Difficult emotions, relationships, and situations provide the most valuable opportunities to choose to be in step with evolution or not. By avoiding, denying, belittling, or rejecting these on any level, you transfer your energy to them, which keeps you disempowered and out of step with evolution.

Therefore, learning to appreciate these difficulties is essential because, otherwise, they become the anchors keeping your boat stuck in the river of evolution.

But how can I appreciate these difficulties?

Imagine for a moment you are in a relationship you feel no longer serves you, (this could be a relationship with a partner, employer, money, situation, health, or relative.)

In fact, the relationship has grown burdensome and painful for you. How easy has it become to hold anger and resentment? How quickly does the truth of your feelings come out in damaging ways? How is your mood affected each day?

What if how you related to this relationship was the connector to not just how the next relationship manifested—but to how the rest of your life unfolded? What if you recognized that your attitude about your now experience affects *everything* coming to you later?

Would this change the way you interact with life?

Feel into this for a moment. Ask, "Is this true? Is the way I relate to my current situation going to impact my next experience and all the experiences afterwards—my entire evolutionary track? Did my life bring me this situation to help me evolve?"

Now, begin to appreciate all the elements and character players in a way that reaches beyond your perceptions of them. Begin to look past the transgressions, the shortcomings, and the hurt feelings to simply appreciate them. Include appreciation for the forces that brought you together, and even those tearing you apart as being perfect for the evolution of everyone.

Furthermore, learn to appreciate the feelings within you that are triggered. In other words, allow yourself to sit with and feel deeply into your feelings without any sort of judgment. Appreciate the feelings as though you are observing some great work of art on the wall of a gallery—being with them as neither good nor bad—just simply as something to be appreciated. Allow your feelings to be heart-felt, and invite the stories your mind is creating to fade.

When you are in willing appreciation of how you feel inside without buying the old story lines, you eradicate your perception of what is there. You discover what you fear, is not real.

What you discover behind every veil of perception is pure energy. And when you remove the container of perception and judgment, this release of energy causes your attractor state to become more infused with the vibration of love—rocketing you forward into your power. This enables you to leave behind what no longer serves you and open to easefully receive what is next in your evolutionary flow.

So, everything required for the evolutionary journey of life simply shows up when you are in active participation by simply being with your feelings.

What You Require To Evolve Shows Up Perfectly As You Are In Step With Evolution.

Being in step is being solidly in the knowing this is the way it works—by perfect design. It is not something to set goals about, nor is it anything to worry or want about—that only spills more of your vital life blood energy and sets you apart from what life wants to give you.

Your responsibility is to see, feel, and play with what shows up with appreciation, rather than fixation. The moment you become fixated, you are into attachment, and you are out of line with the evolutionary energy.

Stay within your integrity as much as possible, and recognize how simple it is to come back into alignment with evolution when you catch yourself out of step.

BE love. That is all that is needed. Love is the connector to all.

Guideline Action One: *Slow Down*
Guideline Action Two: *Love All Feeling.*

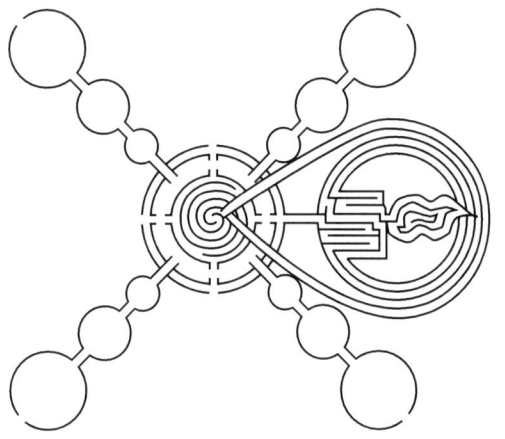

Evolutionary Guideline Three

BE Light.
Light is Light.
Lightness Spreads Light.

Guideline Essence: *Allowance*

Everywhere people are debating and dissecting information, ideas, and opinions as if their lives depended on how serious they were about everything. The ways they relate, dress, act, work, and play are all serious business.

There seems to be little room for playfulness, levity, and transformation.

But is life this serious? Can a different approach help me evolve?

To be an evolutionary means you are constantly making strides to raise *your* personal vibration to come more in step with the energy of evolution. You are raising the vibration of your attractor state by being in a new willingness to say 'yes' to life, and being courageous enough to appreciate those things giving you the most trouble.

It means being willing to step inside each moment and discover what is possible for you through new conscious choices—intuitive choices based in the expanded energy of love rather than the constrictive energy of desire and fear.

It means being willing to become your own personal center for change—an evolutionary force—because you know that no one else can set you free.

To be an evolutionary is to be fully in the flow of life. You are willing to relinquish control of what is happening while remaining conscious of how you interact with what life brings you. You come into a state of *allowance*. You allow what wants to happen to happen. You allow your life to be exactly as it is right now—where you are, how you feel, the quality of your relationships, and the state of your affairs.

You allow things to be the way they are without having to change, manipulate, or judge them, and instead you channel your desire into coming more into alignment with the energy of your heart.

You allow yourself to be a more conscious participant in co-creating your life. You allow people to be exactly who they are, where they are, when they are, and how they are on their evolutionary journeys without having to correct, guide, or give them a better approach.

To come into step with evolution is to ask from deep within to be a vessel for change—to become an evolutionary force through service—and then get out of your way.

How can I be a force of change?

Being a force of evolutionary change does not mean you are forcing change upon anything or anyone.

Actively trying to change someone or debate a situation is out of step with evolution because it comes from a contracted form of energy. By bringing agenda to what you wish to change, you paradoxically reinforce the existing attractor states and add stagnation to the situation through polarity.

Being a true evolutionary is to know the only impact you can have on people is to leave them a little lighter than you found them.

When you engage in a practice of allowing life to come to you and trusting your intuition, you are in alignment with your heart. When you share this inner light, you bring lightness to your surroundings. Apply this practice to any situation in life, and allow what wants to happen to happen - regardless of your agenda.

Imagine for a moment you find yourself with someone or even a group of people who are discussing some cataclysmic occurrence. Imagine them to be fiercely committed to their vision of how events are happening in the world.

Your engagement with this person or group of people leaves an energetic impression upon them.

If you engage them with any debate, anger, or righteousness, they feel validated in their opinions and beliefs because you have matched the energetic tone of what is being discussed and invited them to defend their position.

Furthermore, if you have any strong reaction to what they are discussing, you have, in effect, asked them to extend the dialogue.

However, by staying in the joy of being with fellow human beings and allowing them to be in their experience without agreeing or disagreeing, you have brought a higher vibration into the mix. All you have to do is to be in allowance—to be simply in willingness appreciation of fellow human beings expressing themselves, rather than judging the content of their interaction.

Any engagement they have with you, regardless of the specific dialogue, causes an evolutionary shift when you are authentically present and allow them to be themselves without any interference.

From the view of the evolutionary, there are no fixed points or certain outcomes in an evolving universe. There is always much to be determined, and what is yet to be determined is influenced energetically.

Therefore, always soothe folks so they can open to being less fearful about anything and everything. Choose language that is light and accepting. Share calming ideas and present a vision of higher outcomes than they are imagining.

Be sure to touch people as you greet them. Listen carefully and when you hear or feel fear, joyfully become inquisitive. When you sense someone has a strong agenda to continually and fiercely be in their position regardless of your presence, politely excuse yourself and allow them to be in that space alone.

This is the role of the evolutionary. Your function: to come into step with evolution by raising the vibration of your attractor state, knowing that as you do so others are magically uplifted without your effort but in your presence. The vibration of love is powerful and connects people to their potential.

Be a wave machine of love.

Become such a powerful magnet of peaceful resolution that your truth lights up the darkness in the minds and hearts around you just by your authentic participation.

All you need to do is ask to serve and let evolution take over. Be love and light. This is what pulls you out of the old paradigm and into the new. This is what allows you to be an evolutionary force in your life and in the lives of others.

So what can I do specifically to raise my vibration?

Daily meditative practice is essential. Eat whole foods as much as possible. Live a new model. Treat yourself naturally and subtract any aggression from your exercise. Ride bicycles everywhere. Swim in lakes and oceans. Run laughing in the woods.

Tend to your home and crops with dancing eyes and feet. It is a joyful experience to move your body in service of raising your vibration.

Participate with people in activities that are not competitive and have new outcomes of cooperation that lifts the spirit of everyone.

Bring together or join a group of people to explore creating a *Center for Change* for yourselves and others—a way to passively and peacefully join together to quietly impact the environment around you.

This is simply a pod of folks who have their hearts and minds set on peaceful and abundant outcomes. What part of that is not desired by every human soul? Allow the group to begin exploring how to come into step with evolution together in three ways.

One: Join collectively as individuals to form a regular weekly heart-centered meditation gathering. Set your intention to be in step with evolution and practice being together energetically. Study and apply the Evolutionary Guidelines to raise each individual attractor state. Invite others to join in the process.

Two: Begin exploring with the group ways to impact your community: What social enterprises that espouse evolutionary ideals can be the vehicles for change? How can we assist? What does the evolutionary company look and act like? Build it.

Three: Each of you individually must take responsibility for tuning and turning your body into a temple of evolutionary light by becoming conscious of your language, vision, diet, exercise, and practices. Act as a whole in this endeavor. In other words, be the supporters of one another. Observe what you put into your body and where you place your attention. Are you in-step or out-of-step with evolution.

Be in-step together.

Slow down and be conscious. With what you choose to eliminate, you discover more opportunity to evolve and create. Have fun. This is not about discipline and order. This is about joy and freedom.

Everything you do can have a playful nature to it, for to be in any type of seriousness about this is to be out of your integrity.

When you are in your truth, people want to do and be what and who you are. Make it simple and easy for everyone. Share the joy and ease of it.

BE Light. Light is Light. Lightness Spreads Light.

Allow the light to work its evolutionary magic through you—to penetrate your heart and light the way. Engage in discussions lightly. Excuse yourself from any contradiction of truth in your personal, business and casual conversations. War comes from opposition. Peace comes from compassion. Scolding is out of step.

Loving is in.

Guideline Action One: *Slow Down*
Guideline Action Two: *Love Everything*
Guideline Action Three: *Become Playful*

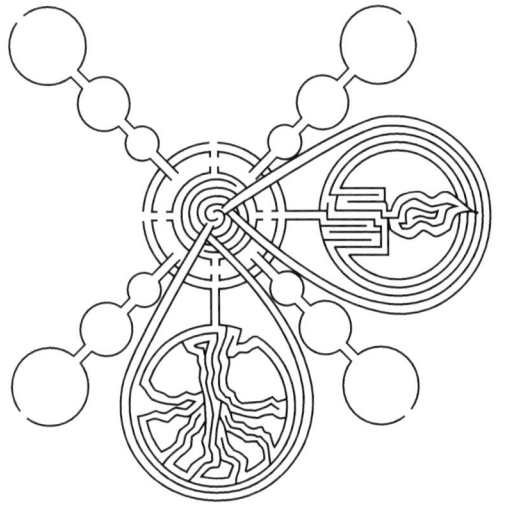

Evolutionary Guideline Four

Be in the Silence.
Silence is the Doorway.
Become a Noise Reducer.

Guideline Essence: *Neutrality*

What is wanted for your life? What does your heart truly desire? Are you letting it in, or are you distracted by how busy and chaotic your life has become?

Many people today are living in fear.

Fear shows up as being apprehensive of the future, clinging to old relationships, being concerned for your children's fate, exercising control over others, worrying about job security, or agonizing about taxation, politicians and the fluctuation in the economy.

To keep ourselves from feeling these fears, we have our lives at full throttle. We distract ourselves with the news, the dramatic lives of other people, stay busy with triviality and succumb to our addictions. We convince ourselves of our self-importance and pack our schedules with perceived obligations. Everywhere we go there is media, something flashing to get our attention, or someone calling to tell us a story. When we get in the car, we make sure that the stereo is on, and the kids are busy with electronic games.

Occasionally we find sleep does not come easily so we medicate ourselves with alcohol or pills to get rest so that we can get up tomorrow and keep spinning plates.

There is a different way to live.

It is time to release the throttle and take our lives out of gear—to find neutrality.

It is perfectly appropriate to have a clear and powerful vision for how you would like your life to become. It is perfectly within your evolutionary right to desire to come into alignment with your highest good. And, it is your destiny to be both self-reliant and connected to a more purposeful life expression.

However, something is in the way.

Something is keeping you out of step with your potential. Something is continually restricting your ability to move beyond challenges regardless of the amount of money or effort thrown at the problems.

Collectively, we have overindulged our individual importance and reasoned our way into a conundrum, ignorant of our interconnectedness through our hearts. We are out of harmony with our emotions. We deny and hide our feelings from view, and yet we are enslaved to them.

Underneath, we are scared and feel lost. We forget that we are in community and refuse to relate to others with similar challenges. We decide to go at it alone, and yet we do not know who we are. We have become what we believe to be fear.

> *If you could listen to the 'fear,'*
>
> *What would the 'fear' tell you?*

Most people mistake fear for rising emotions. What feels like fear is really an indicator of being out of sync with true heart-felt feelings. It is a signal that emotions are surfacing to be expressed, like anger, sadness, jealousy, despair and grief.

Instead, we figure something is either wrong with us or with others, and we stay out of step with evolution.

When we are in the state of resisting what we feel, we busy ourselves to stay distracted from the truth behind the fear, which we imagine to be intolerable and painful.

Despite our attempts to resist them, these emotions are rising in us because of inner change. Behind these feelings is powerful energy attempting to flow through us and add the gift of evolutionary thrust.

The role of the evolutionary, therefore, is to come into harmony with the energy behind the fear by welcoming the emotional change that is percolating to the surface.

The evolutionary engages with the emotion directly by moving in unison with the energy behind the emotion.

So how can I do this?

First of all, when you are stuck in fear or any emotional block, slow down to become aware that you can relate to life differently—you can simply come back into step with evolution.

Secondly, remember everything you are experiencing in your life is okay. It is neither good nor bad. It is neither right nor wrong. It just simply is… neutral. Everything is uniquely your experience and is a part of your evolution, showing up perfectly for your highest good to help you grow. Being with your emotions from a place of neutrality frees up the energy you have been using to keep uncomfortable feelings at bay.

Third, give yourself permission to reduce the noise. Children become balanced emotionally when their parents give them quiet space to express what they are feeling—usually in an episode of crying, sulking, or screaming—rather than trying to stop them from emoting.

Children naturally return to the playful nature of being totally in the moment once the emotional turbulence has passed. They move into the next experience easefully because they are now in balance with what was trying to move through them.

So do the same thing for yourself. What does that mean? Let yourself out of the box of being serious and all grown up—of having it all together. Be okay with being playful with your life, expressing what you feel, and having emotional outbursts. Allow what wants to happen in your feeling body to happen.

Expression > Peace > Flow = Creation

When you are feeling stuck or in fear, the expression of emotion quiets your mind, yielding peace.

When your mind is quiet, the energy of peace gives you thrust in the absence of emotional resistance. This enables you to step into a creative flow once again. The process is about freeing the voice of your intuition from the interference of unexpressed emotion.

For example, a daily journaling practice is an excellent vehicle of expression to help you become adept at creating a manageable flow for releasing emotions, so you can stay in step. Rather than having emotions build up and hold you back, you are now giving them room to flow a little each day.

As an evolutionary, you are continually clearing away this interference to hone your recognition of intuitive feeling. There is always more to discover in this never-ending process. You find being in step with evolution is not about deliberately thinking through the choices in front of you. It is simply about trusting and harmonizing with the flow of energy already happening within you.

Therefore, simply be with what is from a place of neutrality. Be neutral. Just be. If you cannot be neutral, listen to and express what is in the fear until you find peace. Keep going beyond right and wrong. Seek clarity.

Seek silence. Do this even if life is wildly chaotic—especially if it is chaotic.

You want to reach what is on the other side of the chaos of your emotions and thoughts. Become like the eye of the hurricane, and observe the chaos happening around you—emotionally and physically—without spinning around with it.

Become that which is neutral to gain clarity and witness truth.

Often, you can stress over a big question or concern about your life. Ultimately, what decision you make about anything is of little consequence. One choice is never better than another, but one expedites the truth.

The truth always wins out.

What is required always shows up. Evolution always rises to the top. No need to hurry or delay. No need to fear or get too excited.

You are supported in your decisions regardless of what they are. You can always come back into step with evolution even if your intuition is not clear and you find yourself lost. Simply follow the guidelines and make a new choice.

You know when something does not feel right. This is all the reason you need to make any decision. Just keep following the choices that feel right. It is a way to cheat to the truth when you cannot hear the intuitive voice with clarity. Make choices and pay attention to feelings. Your feelings are your guide.

Learn to be still, and find a place of neutrality with your emotions. Learn to listen to the fear from the stillness rather than be swept up in its chaos. Learn to express what you are feeling without getting attached to it being true or false.

Simply let the feelings be what they are—just feelings.

Learn to be in the new stillness after you have expressed the emotion. Listen and feel into the stillness of silence until you hear the whisper of your intuition telling you what to do next. Act with intention. Your results will astound you.

Be in The Silence.

Silence is the Doorway.

Become a Noise Reducer.

Play with this process. Make the choice to be still and quiet. Make the choice to be sane in an insane world, for sanity is only the understanding and implementation of this process of being in neutrality. Sanity is the ability to be yourself in a loud room. It is the determination that your experience is your experience.

It is the understanding that what is coming through your awareness right now is only for you. It may not be what your mind wants, but it is a tonic for your heart.

Drink deep.

Then ride the golden part of the elixir.

Guideline Action One: *Slow Down*
Guideline Action Two: *Love Everything*
Guideline Action Three: *Become Playful*
Guideline Action Four: *Listen to Silence*

Evolutionary Guideline Five

Simplicity Frees Energy.
Simplify Everything.
So Purity Can Work with Purity.

Guideline Essence: *Initiation*

You feel as though you are tiptoeing through life, trying to diligently hold a fragile construct together. There is some hesitancy or indecision about moving beyond the comforts of your life and into step with your evolutionary potential.

Perhaps you have a career paying you well, a relationship too complicated to end, or a traditional family structure that is just comfortable enough to prevent you from commencing on what makes your heart truly sing.

And, when you sit still with yourself late in the evening, you feel unfulfilled and out of sorts with the current trajectory of your life. It appears predictable and irrelevant. Besides, it is getting harder to ignore the beckoning from deep within, which you cannot seem to identify clearly enough to understand. You suspect there is some higher calling for your life, and setting more goals is not going to satisfy you this time. No amount of willpower, no sum of money, or no length of vacation.

Somehow you want to be more fully engaged with life, and you consider rolling the dice to do something unconventional, but what are the risks and for what reward?

You look around.

Everyone else seems to be getting along just fine in this routine. They even seem to enjoy it. "Why can't I just suck it up and keep plodding down the path like them?" you wonder.

So you decide to wait for a better time, until the kids are grown, until there is enough money in the bank, or until the stars line up just right for you to get that tap on the shoulder telling you exactly what to do.

However, you know coasting through life will not do. The perfect time may never come any closer than it is right now. Besides, the feeling in your gut will not leave you alone. The time to sail your boat has come.

Is there another way to live?

What is happening to me and what can I do about it?

What is the gift I am here to share?

Just by being aware of these questions, in a sense, you *have* been tapped on the shoulder. You are being initiated into a different way of living — from the heart.

Evolution has come to your front door and asked for you, only you.

You are starting to notice a richness to life that others do not see or feel, and the conversations you have had for all these years now lack depth and meaning. Your work no longer satisfies you, and you are beginning to suspect the plans you have made were not really yours to begin with — because the predictability and security of them are walling you off from the true nectar of life.

Your heart is opening and with that comes an initiation, a change in awareness. You have a new opportunity to feel your way through life. You suspect the plans you used to make, the rules you used to live by, and the games you used to play will not work any longer.

Stepping into one's evolutionary potential is not a decision. It is neither the result of goal setting nor blind circumstance. It is an initiation of new energy moving through your heart in a new way.

When it happens for you, it happens. There is not much to do about it, except hop aboard your evolutionary boat and be in your heart as fully as you can. Then let go. It is that simple.

Your duty as an evolutionary is to recognize your heart has been heavy, burdened with old emotions obscuring your awareness and anchoring you. You have been coasting through life in order not to feel into the depth of what is inside your heart and lately you have given in to stagnation, frustration, and indecision. Now is the time to become adept at piercing the shield around your heart. This barrier is holding you back from feeling what is emerging in you.

So become a heart shield piercer.

Once you have allowed yourself to really feel and have cleared a path to your intuition, it is time to initiate your journey by moving toward the river of evolution.

It is time to initiate a new vision for your life - a vision of consistency in thought and feeling based in compassion, service, purpose, and light.

You get to decide what you dream about, but this journey is not about control, manipulation, or pre-determination. It is not about competition, rewards, or trophies. Leave all those things behind, for this journey is much, much simpler.

This journey is unlike any you have taken before. This journey is about being totally free in what you dream about and being completely free with what shows up in your dream. All that is required - is for you to decide to get started and get in the boat.

What does it feel like to initiate the journey?

Standing too far back from the river of evolution makes it difficult to feel the flow, so move closer.

Let go of your hesitation and indecision.

The flow does not hurt you even when the water is high. Let the sound of the rushing water, the crackling of the branches as they go down river, and the feeling of negative ions and moisture soothe you. The free flowing elixir of life has the power and intrigue to move you quickly into new places. You can feel it.

You wonder, however, if you can do this journey alone, and yet you stand here by yourself. You are traveling light—no directions, no maps, and no guarantees. You recognize you are leaving a lot behind to get into the boat.

"Am I prepared?" you ask.

Of course, all you need is your authentic self. The time has arrived to ride the feeling of desire. You have much more desire in your heart than you know.

It is time to tap into what you have and to bring it forward for greater benefit. How does your heart's desire want to be expressed? It is up to you to source it from within. Be in your body and be still so your evolutionary guide can direct you.

You are ready. Everything required for the journey is packed. You realize you cannot use anything until you push off from the shore. You feel alone and apprehensive, as well as excited and strangely ready.

Step into the boat and initiate the journey.

You wait for no one, because those who are coming with you are further downstream. You were waiting for them here, even though you did not know them. Did you think they would travel upstream? Were you expecting everything you think you need for the journey to just land on your head where you are now?

Let the water carry you. Let your feeling of desire carry you into the eddy. Let the swirling of the waters be a joyride.

Trust that whatever you need is waiting for you downriver. The river of evolution knows exactly what you require at exactly the right time. The river may change course and the flow may speed up or slow down. The river always takes you to your next destination. The river knows where you are going, even if you do not.

Let go of the shore and grab your oar. Do not paddle; merely keep your boat from getting snagged by the branches. Enjoy swirling and twirling. Laugh out loud. Lie back on the bottom of the boat and stare at the sky through the tips of the trees.

Surrender to the larger will, for it does not serve you to have worry or concern about your journey. The evolutionary journey is a matrix coming together as you move downriver.

So be conscious about what you feel, what you dream, and what you think about. Trust that even though you cannot see beyond the next bend in the river, life experiences are coming together for your greatest evolutionary benefit.

They may bend and curve week to week and day to day, but the flow of the river supports you. You are guided, even when you are out of step and confused. Just use the guidelines to get back into the flow of the river.

Pilot your boat from a place of more feeling and less knowing. Sit and ponder. Be quiet and simple. Be free in your mind and centered in your heart. Be in a simple state of openness to clear the way for newness. New knowledge likes a channel through which to travel.

For example, what if you required something for the journey and it was not with you or in your boat?

Take what you wish for—what you require for the trip—and hold it in your heart with feeling and appreciation.

It would certainly help to ask those who are with you to help you look. If you are alone and want others to help you look, hold them in your heart too. Soon enough, what you require shows up in your field of vision as the river coordinates its course to match your heart-felt vibratory request.

It is that simple; whomever and whatever you require for the journey shows up as you are in step with evolution. Just be sure to initiate the feeling so that the river knows how to support you.

You have made the evolutionary journey too complicated with your mind, and it has grounded you. Go to your heart and get busy.

Simplicity Frees Energy.

Simplify Everything,

So Purity Can Work with Purity.

Be very simple. Be simply basic. The heart has vast organizing power, and the less it has to undo, the better for you. A simple money system. A simple diet. A simple working way. A simple routine. A simple lifestyle. A simple wardrobe. A simple billing system. A simply organized home.

Simplicity frees energy. Others have created tools to make living simple.

Utilize them.

Guideline Action One: *Slow Down*
Guideline Action Two: *Love Everything*
Guideline Action Three: *Become Playful*
Guideline Action Four: *Listen to Silence*
Guideline Action Five: *Become Simple*

Evolutionary Guideline Six

Rapid Acceleration Occurs When People Get into Evolutionary Flow Together.

Guideline Essence: *Efficiency*

If anyone had the ability and the courage to go back in time and visit each and every moment they had been in pain, failed at any endeavor, or experienced turmoil - they would find in each situation, they were terrifically and terribly alone.

They would find they created stories to warrant their feelings and justify their reactions. They would find that just at the moment they needed someone to reflect the truth back to them, they dove deeper into the illusion of separateness. They would be amazed to discover, in fact, they had been completely responsible for each and every episode.

And they would be in awe of just how amazingly powerful their ego had been in each situation in maintaining the illusion and keeping them from their heart.

Being human is to be at the mercy of the entrapment of this illusion while life is happening—to believe so strongly we are separate from all that is around us, that we cannot see or experience it any other way.

This experience of separateness keeps us stuck in our old patterns.

Evolutionary Guideline One refers to the popular view of the law of attraction as a means to get what one wants by altering one's attractor state.

From this perspective, we are out of step with evolution because we believe we can control what is happening around us. This creates and cements the illusion of separateness.

On the other hand of the evolutionary perspective, the law of attraction is simply a way to explain the evolutionary force surrounding us. It is a force of consciousness that continually brings to us what mirrors our soul's desire to evolve — our vibration.

Everything we need to utilize, transcend, and relate to on our evolutionary journey just shows up and does so because we are one with it. We are not separate.

Life is already happening to us perfectly.

The path of the evolutionary is not to try and make sense of the illusionary world, conspire how to win the game, or escape its clutches. The path is to simply accept the playground in which you live and seek to fully experience it through an open heart. It is through the heart that one experiences the inner-connectivity of everything.

Look around you and see how many people are in pain and suffering because they are experiencing themselves as individuals rather than as integral to the larger whole. Cultivate compassion for them and choose to experience life as magical and mystical while being in conscious relationship with the people in your life—all of them.

Humans evolving together with humility is in step with evolution because it takes a collective to clearly see through the entanglements of each individual illusion. Why try and get out of a hedge maze by yourself, when it is more efficient to do so with a partner or group?

How can I be in conscious evolutionary relationships?

It always starts with you. Become more conscious that every relationship is an evolutionary relationship with the sole purpose of being a catalyst for your evolution.

Every relationship is born out of the merging of the individual attraction energies to present opportunities for everyone to come into step with evolution or not. The more powerful the energy bringing people and situations together, the more potent the evolutionary forces at play and the more thrust available for your evolution.

All relationships have a honeymoon period where the natural attracting energies outweigh any other feelings while the relationship is being formulated. Later, when the attraction begins to wane, the connection reveals entanglements that seem to be out of the spirit of what you think the relationship should be like.

You used to enjoy being with this person (or situation), and now they are driving you crazy and difficulties are surfacing.

This is where you have to use your evolutionary practices to slow everything down enough to follow the Evolutionary Guideline Process.

First, be in *willingness* to recognize that the current blame, hurt feelings, or volatility is not a problem or anyone's fault, but simply an opportunity to evolve. See that you attracted this relationship to transcend whatever difficulties are being presented and be willing to accept your responsibility.

Second, be in *appreciation* of all the people involved (including you), and the incredible forces that have placed you together. Look beyond the personalities to see the perfection of everyone's soul connection to recognize this opportunity to demonstrate a higher outcome.

Third, step into *allowance* so that what wants to happen can happen. Bring lightness to the situation and get your agenda out of the way to allow the relationship to naturally come back into balance.

Fourth, be in *neutrality* with your emotions to step beyond the storylines and disengage from the drama so the essence of what is bubbling up to serve the situation can surface. Create space for whatever truth is emerging.

Finally, there must be an *initiation* of wholeness. It is very simple at this point. It is time to deeply feel what is now present in you so it can be safely expressed and you can evolve. In this moment, all resistance is obliterated as new pathways emerge to travel that were previously obscured from your awareness.

You always have freewill choice to let go of what does not serve your evolutionary journey, to disengage. By doing so you change the nature of all your relationships going forward as you attract more conscious journeyers.

Now, imagine for a moment that using this process has uncovered anger (or any emotion) in you. This anger, which may have inspired you to create stories with no real foundation in your relationships, now has no seemingly good reason behind it.

You know this anger was simply brought to the surface to be jettisoned rather than to create additional drama, but you are having a difficult time letting go.

"What about this anger in me?"

Your anger is okay. Let it be what it is. What is always wanted for your life is heart harmony so you can fully be in your life's potential. So let the anger be and drop into life without it. Let what you are angry about be. It is tricky. You cannot deny or react to what you feel (the anger), or it will puncture your evolutionary boat.

Saying, "Wow, I'm angry." to someone without placing blame might just be enough. Acknowledgement is sometimes enough to relieve you of the load. So move it—using your evolutionary practices—out of the boat, so you are not sinking or floating heavy in the water.

The old way you lived in relationship to emotions had its own navigation system, which does not work well in the evolutionary river. You are now into a lighter and more freeing type of navigation. Not in control but powerfully in charge of your energy, attention and quality of your intent. Control is a lot to give up, a lot to let go of. Let it go. It does not work downstream anyway.

Disengage from the anger and refocus your attention on the journey. As you float down the river new people show up. They are different from those whom you have associated with before, and your interaction is unlike earlier relationships for your connection is based in the heart. They may cause you to question whether you are in the right boat.

They may cause you to question everything - not for any reason, but for the way you feel in their presence.

This is your marker that you have met a person who is to accompany you on the next phase of your journey down the river.

Trust the flow of the river, and be open to new experiences so you can accept who is coming to help you on your journey. Pay attention and stay in your heart. Be present with your feelings and listen to your intuitive voice. Have faith in the energy that moves you toward wholeness.

When you come together with your evolutionary partner(s), take time each day to reveal the next steps of your journey. Utilize a meditation practice to create space for the energy between you to flow unencumbered by emotions or thought.

Be present together from the standpoint of service to a larger mission. Simply be together in the existing energy and each rest in the question of: *"How May I Serve?"*

Release individual needs and dive into the meditation freely from the standpoint of serving what wants to happen.

When you find the relationship blocked by fear, sadness, jealousy, or personal agenda, utilize the Evolutionary Guideline Process to release the blocks and make the next evolutionary step.

Be open to your evolutionary partnerships being in a state of flux just like everything else. Allow your intuition and feelings to guide your choices. Trust your magic.

The energy of the collective connection is far more powerful than what anyone can do alone. It is a vortex. The vortex is a creative force connecting the partnership to everything in the seen and unseen worlds with tremendous efficiency.

Just like your own attractor state, the energy of the vortex cannot simultaneously be manipulated and remain in step with evolution.

You participate by simply feeling the energy and allowing it to bring forth what wants to happen—first in feeling, and then into form.

You may feel a little uneasy at first with this new way of being in partnership. Part of resting in service to a larger mission is to both learn how to become comfortable and adept in utilizing the process. Hesitation only thwarts the process and keeps you feeling out of sync, as does any hastening. Go ahead and dive into the feelings in your heart and intuitively act when the choice becomes choice-less. Everything your heart wants for you, is provided. It just shows up. Keep applying the Evolutionary Guidelines.

Working from heart space diligently with clarity and enthusiasm together is a powerful moving force formulating the direction of the river for everyone involved in ways you cannot see, understand, or even explain.

Now is not the time to convince yourself of that. Now is the time to give yourself the experience.

Within evolutionary relationships you interweave multiple rivers of light to create an expansive mosaic unencumbered by normal interference. All these individual life streams are running concurrently and are intertwined to affect consciousness in a way that elevates the entire planet and all of her inhabitants.

You join rivers and streams that are consciously flowing and carrying more light of a higher frequency. They run with more fluidity and are not dammed up and polluted like the old rivers flowing below. These are filled with light and flowing above the fields and mountains, washing clean everything below with something unseen but profoundly impactful.

Do not worry, therefore, about the old, the bad, and the ugly. They are being undone by a new level of consciousness—by evolution itself—in ways that only countless rivers of pure clean waters of light can do.

Rapid Acceleration Occurs

When People Get into Evolutionary Flow Together.

Stop questioning. Finalize your plan of action through your intuitive processes each day, and take conscious action to move over and beyond the blockages downstream. Rivers flow many courses.

You are working with a five-dimensional scope. You might still be living in a land of three-dimensional barriers, but your river runs beyond what is experienced by the five senses into a larger holistic evolutionary field. Yes, it is a big leap. Take it. Use it. Show it to others. It is simply more efficient.

Guideline Action One: *Slow Down*
Guideline Action Two: *Love Everything*
Guideline Action Three: *Become Playful*
Guideline Action Four: *Listen to Silence*
Guideline Action Five: *Become Simple*
Guideline Action Six: *Connect Hearts*

Evolutionary Guideline Seven

Dive Into the Mystery —
Into Not Knowing —
And Become What Wants to Happen.

Guideline Essence: *Nothingness*

What wants to happen? What if every day you choose to spend time with this question and open to new possibilities? What if every day is new, exciting, and unpredictable? How delicious can life become?

What wants to happen? Exactly what is happening out there! Out in nature, beyond the horizon, and into the stars. It is what is happening without any interference of thinking, planning, agenda, format, or construct. Throw away your plans. Disregard your ideas.

Forget what you know and sit in a place of innocent nothingness and get to *What Wants to Happen.*

What does want to happen? Who wants to be in your skin? What wants to be born in your life? What wants to be invented to serve many in their evolution? What new paradigm wants to be brought up through the vortex to serve humanity?

Play and joyfully spin in this delicious question. Dive in with the people around you. Dive into the ecstasy of your heart, right here, right now.

What wants to happen!?! What wants to happen as you open the vortex by laughing and giggling and dancing?

To evolve you must become evolution itself—a dance of intertwining purpose and function and newness and light and movement. Forget the way things have been done before. Throw away what has happened, and get into evolution. Get into the mystery.

Does anyone know what is happening in our ecology? No. Scientists have many theories. But what is really happening is beyond the human mind. It is beyond any fabric you have ever rested upon. It is something to surrender to and merge with.

Let go of who you think you have been and become what you are wanted to be.

Your soul purpose is not something predetermined in the way you imagine. The reason it is a hard question for people to answer is that the expression of soul purpose is ever changing and ever moving because of evolution.

Love has many outlets, and once you give yourself permission to be in service to love, anything becomes possible.

Yes, some people come to earth and do one thing their entire lives. But that is not you.

Your eyes are dancing. You want to dive into the deliciousness of your life. You are waiting for someone to give you permission to act in the way your heart desires. You are waiting for someone to tell you it is okay to dance on Sunday in the street with a hat on.

You are waiting for the inner knowingness that it is okay to walk into your oppressive job and hug and love on your controlling boss and say, "Thank you, thank you, thank you. Thank you for showing me what not to do. I love you!!! I love you!!! Thanks to you I have money and I learned these things and . . . My, what a beautiful man you are!! I never noticed before. Well anyway, I came in to tell you that. And goodbye!!"

Or simply show up one day and be so blazing happy you infect everyone with love and purpose. Become the force of heart that either changes the culture of the company or forces them to fire you for spreading too much joy and happiness.

It is clear to you most of the world is sleepwalking. So as an evolutionary and as an agent of the heart, unwind the tension in every room you enter. Unwind the matrix supporting the people walking in their sleep. Unwind the fabric in such a way that people are propelled into new places.

It is okay; you can do this—all of it. Act from an intuitive place. Do it from a place of integrity of heart. Do it because it is your divine way of being in the world. There is no reason to be reckless. When in the integrity of the heart, let the heart do the work and leave your agenda out of it.

When you are in *Nothingness*, you become one part of an infinite mosaic of a Self-Organizing Field, a divine matrix of potential being expressed through your experience.

Be in nothingness by staying committed to your meditative practices, the Evolutionary Guidelines, and your evolutionary relationships to bring what wants to happen to light. And then to life.

Leave behind those who are unwilling to come with you. Go where they are not yet willing to travel. What is waiting for you is far more magical than the places of safety where you have harbored.

Go into the places others find uncomfortable, those places you know you must travel. Your passage into these places is what makes the journey worthwhile for others to initiate.

The world is asking for more evolutionary guides - more people living with true compassion from an open heart.

It is okay to tear up the script of your life and speak from the heart. When you know nothing, you stand fully in your power. This is your destiny; your purpose. Go share it, and dive into the mystery of nothingness.

Remember, your experience is real. Everyone's experience is real. Therefore, never discount anyone's experience, and never throw seeds of doubt onto anyone's plate. Always speak of possibility. Always speak of hope. Always speak of resolution, reconciliation, reformulation, purpose, and possibility.

Dogs have it right in a lot of ways. Wag your tail!

Dive Into The Mystery —

Into Not Knowing,

And Become What Wants To Happen.

Become what is Choosing to be Born in the Moment—

What Before this Moment did not Exist.

Guideline Action One: *Slow Down*
Guideline Action Two: *Love Everything*
Guideline Action Three: *Become Playful*
Guideline Action Four: *Listen to Silence*
Guideline Action Five: *Become Simple*
Guideline Action Six: *Connect Hearts*
Guideline Action Seven: *Dive Deeply*

Seven is the completion of Nothing in the understanding that Nothing gives Birth to Everything and grants all wishes through the Self-Organizing Field of Divine Love.

Introduction to Guideline Eight

Open to Something New

Essence: *Mystery*

In 2009, the Seven Evolutionary Guidelines presented themselves to MysterE through a series of seven lucid energy dreams. He was able to transcribe the transmissions as they came through him in the middle of the night by translating the energy into English as he typed it into his smartphone.

Recognizing this material as being intuitively from him, and yet foreign to him, he began to study, practice and radically live in the truth of these words, initiating a humbling journey into the heart of mysticism, magic, serendipity, grace and heart-broken openness for a greater sense of personal empowerment and embodiment of soul purpose and service.

The "you" language of the text is exactly how he received the information, and it is shared not as a directive from MysterE to you, but as a directive from MysterE to himself.

Now in 2016, at the age of 49, MysterE is sharing an eighth guideline which came through the experience of living the first seven as a daily practice for the past seven years.

The first seven guidelines remain unchanged, however are slightly refined for a more efficient embodiment by the reader.

Enjoy the Eighth Guideline.

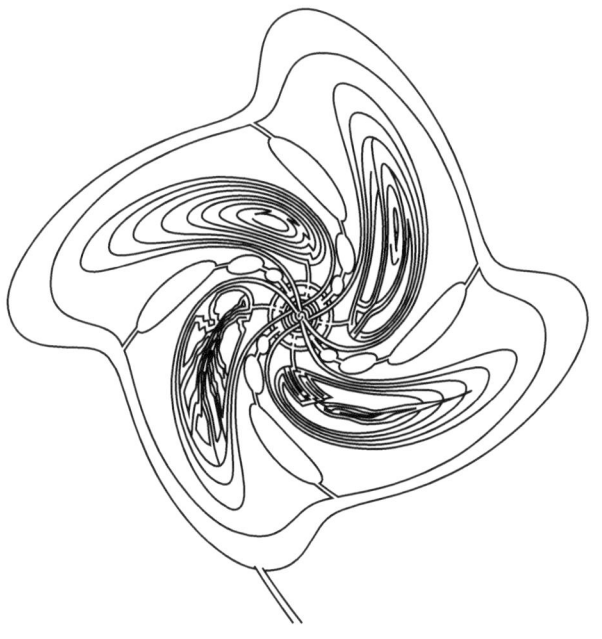

Evolutionary Guideline Eight

See Perfection Now —
For Only Perfection Exists.
What is Happening Now is
Divine Orchestration.

Guideline Essence: *Alchemy*

Raise your right hand, place your left hand over your heart and repeat the following intention out-loud: "I am an alchemist, a life artist. I am powerfully choosing to divinely co-create my life authentically from my heart."

Once you recognize yourself as always choosing

everything in your experience whether you are aware of the choice or not, there isn't much room left to be in resistance to what is… the… truth… of… your… life…

Yes, you are a Divine Co-Creator. You've always been powerfully in charge of your life, and you have always received exactly what you've given yourself. You are simply becoming more aware of this truth now.

Own it. Choose it. Become it. Embody it. Share it. Whatever it takes to expand your desire to become stronger than your resistance. Dive in with whatever life is bringing to you that feels in alignment with your truth and give yourself a release from everything else. Embodiment of this truth is necessary for your spiritual growth and enlightenment.

Evolutionary Guideline 8 – Alchemy – is the result of choosing to learn and practice the seven original guidelines as an alchemic formula to bring your awareness to a place of empowerment through radical self-compassion; over and over and over, until you embody the ability to be in divine love regardless of circumstance. It is simply the formula for healing and manifesting through an open heart.

The alchemy of compassion is the ability to be so powerfully present and in love with what is happening, that all your ideas, traumas, stories and fantasies collapse into one life experience of empowerment and self-expression.

As an evolving human and emerging evolutionary guide, you are inviting yourself to learn how to transmute suffering, by learning how to grieve, how to feel, how to be soft and open, and how to be humble and compassionate with yourself in every moment. Therefore, living the greatest of all paradoxes: You are powerful beyond measure in your vulnerability.

You are learning a compassionate person's attained power therefore becomes a vehicle for service to humanity through personal transformation and the sharing of your emerging gifts.

You are learning to accelerate your evolution into wholeness by bringing all the character aspects you have played in this and many lifetimes into one now expression.

You are learning how to be with yourself so innocently, that you dismantle all perceptions of being separate from God.

You are learning that slowing down the mind and opening the heart to feeling is simple - and yet is no easy task. However, it is the mastery of this simplicity that unravels your perception from illusion and brings you back into the truth of your existence.

You are learning courageously and outrageously to become more authentic. Yes, be more like you. Let yourself be your Self. Get to know yourself by loving the totality of your entire life experience.

You are learning to untangle understanding by loving your way through your challenges until you can feel the perfection of every moment and be completely present with your experience in your original wholeness – your inner childlike innocence, which is maturity. Not maturity in the sense of being grown up, but maturity in the sense of being completely responsible for the life you are creating; all of it.

You are invited to sit in meditation and use your inner vision to bring forth all the characters you have played into the center of your awareness ... the narcissist, the hero, the bum, the fool, the lover, the villain, the queen, the peasant, the victim, the perpetrator and others. Bring them into your heart with absolute self-compassion. Allow your true Self to be the center beam of awareness to witness and shine pure light upon all fragments and facets of your consciousness with a new willingness to say yes to all aspects of yourself with love.

Let go of seeing your life as peaks and valleys of imagined success and failure. Let go of the stories that 'this was good' and 'that was bad.' Let go of all the moral judgments you have about you that are right, wrong, good or bad. Let go of any and all ideas that there is something to fix, control or improve, and begin to appreciate everything – all of it – all of life – as it is – in every moment. Practice this until your heart feels light and forgiving.

Now, from this awareness, allow yourself to recognize the mystery of your life and alchemy of every moment as simply being the formula of who you are now. Every single event of your life is essential to who you are, and are becoming.

See how you are continually waking yourself up by bringing these formally segregated parts of yourself back together through bouts of self-imposed contrast to get your attention of the healing which is wanting to happen.

See therefore, how every time you emerge from a bout of suffering or dis-ease in the illusion, that eventually in hindsight, you are able to see your experiences as vital to your spiritual path.

Playfully celebrate the reunion of your soul, the

reunion of your selves, the reunion of your identity as pure and divine. Have the courage, as well, to see the perfection of your experience and bless all occurrences as being perfect as they are happening now, rather than coming to that awareness later.

Furthermore, have the audacity to recognize the entire play of consciousness as perfectly perfect — to see the vastness of perfection in the ocean of imperfection, and to be brave enough and free enough to be amused by your follies instead of reprimanding yourself for imagined wrong doings.

You are simply waking yourself up to see your self-imposed prison does not exist – that you have been the warden with the keys to your freedom all along. And in its complete absurd imperfection, life is completely perfect because it is what is — a mirror of your own projected consciousness, which is of course, perfectly perfext.

Be in such a radical allowance of your Divine Creator that you are able to look into the heavens and into every person's eyes you meet, and say, "I am doing this... all of this... I am completely responsible for my life, and it's absolutely perfect in the imperfection that it is!"

Yes.

Powerfully hold this vision of perfection to distill your perception of imperfection until only purity exists and a *frequency of trust* is established in your Heart — based on your truth, rather than in the truth of others.

See Perfection Now —
For Only Perfection Exists —
What is Happening Now is Divinely Orchestrated.

The *frequency of trust* is one of complete compassion. It is free of shame, guilt and lust. It is firmly rooted in service to humanity with an open heart, exhibiting that all is provided for now, for everyone, for all times. It is also anchored in the knowing that by simply acknowledging what wants to happen, we bring it into form.

Holding a vision of perfection, inspires you and others to make an evolutionary leap to bring creativity and compassion to the way you live life for a more peaceful abundant existence for all.

The Evolutionary Guidelines give us a formula for a powerful alchemy that allows us to transform the darker, condensed, and hidden aspects of our consciousness into expressions for our empowerment.

As you practice and master this alchemy, it becomes a way of living in the moment rather than something you are learning through experience. Very quickly, what took you years or months to transcend, now happens easefully, as you learn to become far more efficient in your ability to heal and create by simply being in your heart.

So, to what vision are you committed?

The destiny of your life and humanity has yet to be

determined, and yet the ultimate outcome for everyone is to evolve into love. It is the ultimate paradox, again. It is truly a hall of mirrors, as all paths lead to the same place. When you embody this truth, there are no dead ends or wrong turns - only twists and turns leading you back to the center of your heart.

Yes, life becomes a labyrinth and a most fantastical playground — and when realize you can shift your experience of reality with the levers of your heart, then anything becomes possible simply through the altering of perception through radical self-compassion.

But you must choose powerfully to see it this way or miss receiving the gift. You must commit every fiber of your being to dismantling your self-inflicted old ways of thinking, feeling and reacting.

This is the portal you are entering now. The portal every human being enters in this life or after. It seems scary. It looks dangerous. It sounds preposterous. Nothing feels safe anymore. However, because when you are anchored in a *frequency of trust*, and you follow your heart's guidance, everything turns out better than you could have planned.

Each one of us chooses a new reality by seeing perfection now. Not later. Not as soon as you get evidence that it's going to work out. Not when you get the gift. No, we are co-creating a new reality by aligning ourselves with the frequency of trust. So…

See Perfection Now.

Be Your Gift.

Imagine the Impact.

Feel the frequency of trust. Open your heart's desire to grow. Treat yourself as a garden. Become so in line with your true Self, there is nothing left to grow but love. When the desire to be free grows beyond your resistance, change happens immediately, ease-fully, compassionately and magically.

If you want a better world, go beyond what you see and experience, to create what your heart truly desires — from within. Yes, it is time to trust your magic and demonstrate how everything comes from nothing.

Now…

Be Like You.

Love Your Way Though.

Enjoy Your Destiny.

Guideline Action One: *Slow Down*
Guideline Action Two: *Love Everything*
Guideline Action Three: *Become Playful*
Guideline Action Four: *Listen to Silence*
Guideline Action Five: *Become Simple*
Guideline Action Six: *Connect Hearts*
Guideline Action Seven: *Dive Deeply*

Guideline Action Eight: *Trust Your Magic*

Seven Labyrinths
for One Portal of Awakening

In 2014, MysterE was asked to design a labyrinth that incorporated symbols from traditional religions, ancient spirituality and the emerging compassionate consciousness to allow people of all backgrounds to appreciate the human journey of faith and initiate awakenings of Divine Love.

Represented here are the four directions, the four elements and four universal spiritual pillars; faith, action, love and grace. Also represented is the cross, seven chakras, flower of life and the soul of human awareness.

Our vision is to make these labyrinths available for people all over Earth to enjoy and experience themselves as part of the greater whole for a more compassionate existence for all.

Please see: www.lifeisheart.com/labyrinths.

Thank You for Your Experience of Reading

*To listen to MysterE read this book,
or visit the River House MysterE School,
please see: www.lifeisheart.com.*

Other Books by MysterE on Amazon:

Give Her What She Wants
The Gift is Listening

In Gratitude:

For all the characters who buzz in and out of the River House MysterE School exhibiting the courage and vulnerability to be in the freedom of their full expression. You are the true inspiration.

Made in United States
Orlando, FL
30 May 2023

33631261R00072